EUROPE

ASIA

AFRICA

PACIFIC OCEAN

INDIAN OCEAN

OCEANIA

ANTARCTICA

Titles in this series

Animal Alphabet Book
Birds
Plants
Animals
Animal Homes

The publishers would like to thank the staff of World Wildlife Fund
for their help in making these books.

Acknowledgment:
Front and back cover and endpaper illustrations by Stephen Lings.

LADYBIRD BOOKS, INC.
Auburn, Maine 04210 U.S.A.
© LADYBIRD BOOKS LTD 1988
Loughborough, Leicestershire, England
Panda logo © 1986 Copyright WWF – International
Printed in England

WORLD WILDLIFE FUND
Plants

written by GILLIAN DORFMAN
illustrated by SHEILA GALBRAITH

Ladybird Books

Produced in association with World Wildlife Fund

There are many different kinds of plants, all over the world.

Some grow in rocky places.

These plants grow near water.

Some g

4

How do plants live? How do they grow?

...oodlands.

Some grow in jungles.

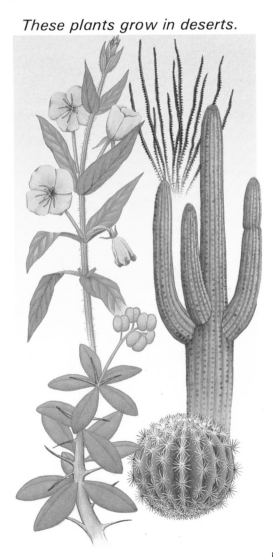

These plants grow in deserts.

5

Most plants grow from seeds.

The seed lies under
the ground.

When the sun shines
and warms the ground,
and when rain falls and
soaks the soil, the
seed begins to grow.

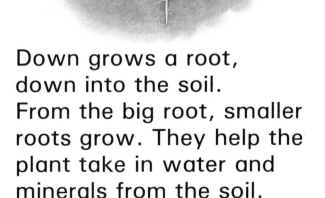

red campion

Down grows a root,
down into the soil.
From the big root, smaller
roots grow. They help the
plant take in water and
minerals from the soil.

Up grows a shoot,
up toward the sun.
Green leaves grow from
the shoot. The seed has
become a young plant.

The young plant grows. It gets bigger and bigger. All day the leaves are busy making food for the plant. They need water and minerals from the soil and air to make food.

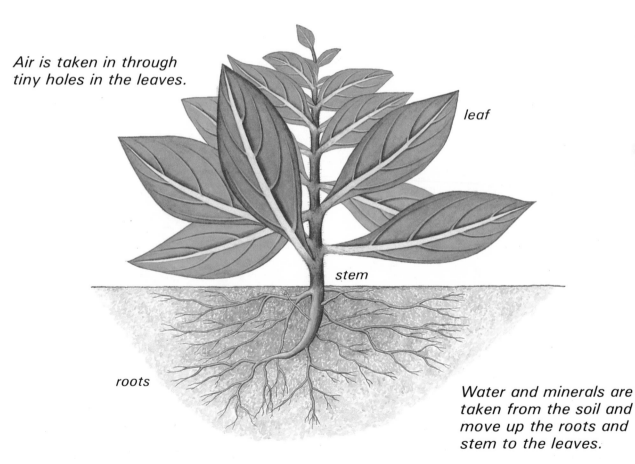

Air is taken in through tiny holes in the leaves.

leaf

stem

roots

Water and minerals are taken from the soil and move up the roots and stem to the leaves.

The green leaves grow out toward the sun.
The leaves and the sun work together, turning
water and minerals from the soil, and air from all
around, into food. The plant
needs food to grow.

The buds on the plant open into
flowers.

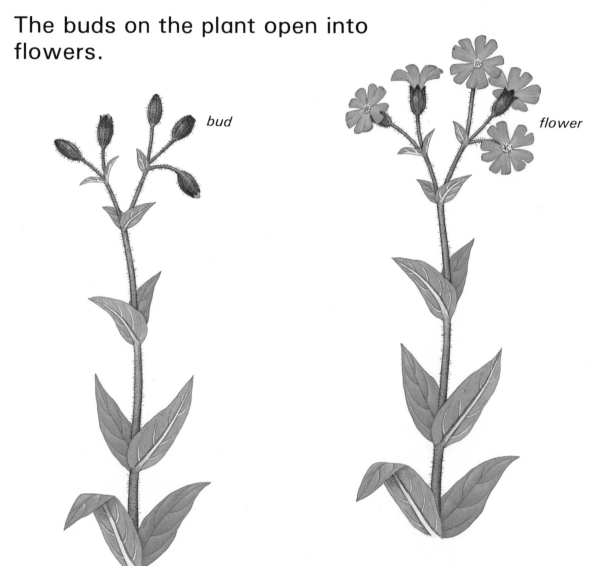

bud

flower

The flowers will make seeds.

Bees buzz from one flower to another. They help the flowers make seeds. Sometimes the wind helps flowers make seeds, too.

*The bee stops on one flower to look for food. It finds sweet juice called **nectar**, and yellow dust called **pollen**. Some of the pollen sticks to the bee's body.*

When the bee moves to another flower, some of the pollen falls off its body. The flower uses this pollen to make seeds.

The wind helps these grasses make seeds. Grass pollen is so light the wind blows it from one plant to another.

blackberry

As the seeds on this plant grow, the flowers wither and die.

Only the part holding the seeds is left. Slowly it grows and swells to become the fruit.

Soon the fruit is ripe,
and a hungry bird eats it
— seeds and all!

Later these seeds fall to
the ground in the bird's
droppings.

13

Seeds can be carried
to new growing places
by animals...

...or by wind.

*Burdock seeds have special
hooks that catch on the fur of
animals as they brush past.*

*Dandelion seeds have their own little
"parachutes" to carry them in the wir*

Some seeds are scattered by water.

And some plants scatter their own seeds.

Waves from the sea wash these coconut seeds ashore.

When the seeds of the wood sorrel are ripe, the pods burst, scattering the seeds.

Some seeds may fall on rocks, where they cannot grow. But this coconut seed has been washed onto soil, where the sun will warm it and the rain will soak it, and it will grow into a new plant.

The coconut seed has its own store of food, which will feed the growing plant until it has put down roots and sprouted shoots and leaves. Then it can make its own food.

Each kind of plant is special, and grows in its own special way. Some plants grow fast. Others grow slowly.

A daisy grows fast, but an oak tree takes years and years to grow.

17

Beech trees are big plants.

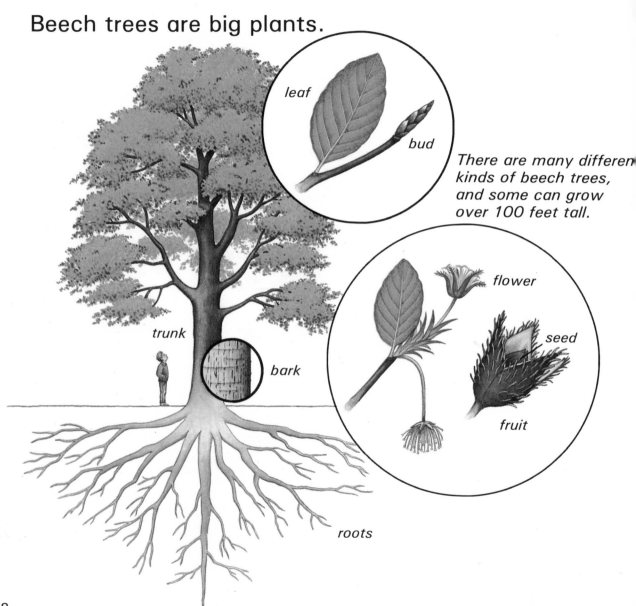

leaf

bud

trunk

bark

roots

flower

seed

fruit

There are many different kinds of beech trees, and some can grow over 100 feet tall.

Poppies and buttercups
are little plants.

flower

bud

leaf

roots

19

There are green plants, and some that are not green.

This bracket fungus is a plant,
but it is not green.
It cannot make its own food.
It feeds on this tree stump.

There are plants with flowers, and some with no flowers at all.

These are not flowering plants.
This pine tree has cones.
Inside the cones are seeds.

Fungi and ferns make tiny
spores instead of seeds.
The spores explode from
the plant and land in new
places where they can grow.

cone

spores

Each kind of plant grows in its own special place. Some grow in hot, dry places...

In this hot desert, there is little rain.
When rain falls,
these cacti take up
as much water as they can
through their roots
and store it in their stems.
Then they can live for
a long time without rain.

...and others grow in cold, windy places.

Mountain plants are small,
so the wind cannot blow them over.

moss campion

gentian

Some plants grow on land...

yellow
iris

Most plants grow
in soil. Their roots keep
them firmly in place.

forget-me-not

24

...and some grow in water.

reeds

arrowhead

This duckweed floats on water.

water lily

Sometimes plants live alone, and sometimes they live with many other plants. Here is a jungle, where many different plants live together.

Swiss cheese plant

snake plant

Each kind of plant is different. But nearly all plants
need food and water, air and sun. If a plant
has these things, it can feed, grow, and make
new plants. It can live.

WWF

Many of our world's plants and animals
are in danger. People have destroyed or polluted the
places in which they live or grow. Some animals
have been hunted until every one of them has been
killed. This is what happened to the dodo, an
amazing flightless bird that once lived in Mauritius.
The same thing could happen to gorillas, tigers, and
whales unless we do something to save them now.

WWF (World Wildlife Fund) was set up to warn people
about the dangers threatening the earth's wildlife.
If we know and care about what happens to
our world, we may be able to protect it
before too much damage is done.

World Wildlife Fund
Membership Dept. LB89
1250 24th Street N.W.
Washington, D.C. 20037